BY

Will Hanafin

This Edition published in 2007 by
Merlin Publishing
Newmarket Hall,
Cork Street, Dublin 8
Ireland
www.merlinwolfhound.com

First Edition © 2001 Will Hanafin
Text © 2007 Will Hanafin
Editing, design and arrangement © 2007 Merlin Publishing
except
Cartoons by Aongus Collins

ISBN 978-1-903582-73-2

Hanafin, Will
De Little Book of Bertie
1. Ahern, Bertie, 1951-
2. Prime ministers – Ireland
I. Title
941.7′0824′092

Typeset by Gough Typesetting Services, Dublin
Printed and bound by J.H. Haynes & Co. Ltd., Britain
Cover Design by Artwerk Design
Cover Photograph by McCarthy Photography
All rights reserved. No part of this publication may be
reproduced, transmitted, or stored in a retrieval system of any
kind without the permission of the publisher.

Contents

Noughty Bertie

Bertie-isms

Bertie and Haughey

The Ahern Years 1

What He Said... Rough Translations

Just what the hell is he talking about?

Bertie's Inner Self

The Ahern Years 2

The World According to Celia

The Ahern Years 3

DIY Bertie Speech-Making 1

DIY Bertie Speech-Making 2

Other Famous Bertie's

Noughty
Bertie

I HATE WHEN THEY FIGHT!

"This is not good. The meeting was bad. Relations were bad. It was very hostile, even bitter........I don't like to see grown men bickering."

(Referring to an EU budget meeting)

Sunday Independent • 19 June 2005

BLESSED IS THE BERTIE

"I don't feel I need to own a huge house with a huge glasshouse when I can go down the road 10 minutes and visit the Botanic Gardens. It's just the way I think about things."

The Irish Times • 13 November 2004

COMRADE BERTIE

*"I am one of the few socialists
left in Irish politics."*

The Irish Times • 13 November 2004

SOCIALIST PARTY POOPER

"If Bertie Ahern is a socialist the moon is a balloon, Ian Paisley is a member of Opus Dei and Tony Blair never told a lie."

(Socialist Eamon McCann dismissing his new comrade Bertie)

Business and Finance • 16 December 2004

CHAIRMAN MOAN!

"I'm well paid so I can't moan. But if I hadn't got that I wouldn't moan too much either."

The Irish Times • 13 November 2004

RICH MAN POOR MAN

"There is a concern that we have become more materialistic, maybe even more selfish, and if we have, I believe many people would conclude that, for all our new wealth, we are much the poorer."

Sunday Independent • 17 September 2006

PEACEFUL TRANSITION

"It was just that a few people believed that I was supporting the war. I was always dead against the war. I did all I could throughout to hold and uphold the UN position. That's why I said that 100,000 people who marched were supporting me."

(Talking about the Government's 'anti-war' stance on Iraq)

Irish Independent • 27 December 2003

NOW WHERE DID THEY GET THAT IDEA?

"Any such change at this time could be seen by the United States and its allies as the adoption of a hostile position in relation to their country and their interests."

(Dáil debate on the use of Shannon Airport)

Irish Independent • 22 March 2003

"We have a relationship with the US. I think we've had that understanding for a long way back. For us to withdraw something that's been there since 1955 was not something I was prepared to do."

The Irish Times • 22 March 2003

ABOUT TIME!

"It is clear that there have been huge failures in US policy towards Iraq."

Irish Independent • 21 January 2007

END OF AN ERA

"I sold the anorak in the end. It was auctioned to raise money for a school, and it went for a small fortune."

The Sunday Times • 14 May 2006

YELLOW FEVER!

"The cut of his suit is perfect. It is a pleasure to see a mature man wear his grey hair so well. All in all, a perfect leader."

(A Mexican newspaper on his style
at the G8 Summit gathering)

Irish Independent • 3 July 2004

YELLOW PERIL!

"I was there with Putin, Chirac and Bush, so I had no chance – I had to stand out some way. Now everyone remembers the jacket and no-one remembers the meeting."

(The reasoning behind his fashion choices at the G8 Summit)

The Sunday Times • 14 May 2006

NOT WORTH THINKING ABOUT!

"I'm still with Celia. At least that's who I was in bed with last night."

Sunday Tribune • 21 July 2002

ALTERNATIVE ENERGY

"Thank God I have huge energy. I'm still putting in 80 hours a week."

Sunday People • 10 April 2005

MERE MORTAL

"I've lots of abilities, but I can't drive the Japanese economy."

Irish Independent • 7 June 2003

WRITE ON!

"We are not high up on the league of pencils."

(Arguing for electronic voting because
of our high-tech industries)

Sunday Tribune • 9 May 2004

FINANCIAL GURU!

"We cannot spend what we have not got."

The Irish Times • 16 November 2002

ONE HOUR PHOTO

"I'll do a FAS course on fixing them."

(Reacting to news that it takes eight
months to fix speed cameras)

Sunday People • 1 May 2005

THE GREATEST AMERICAN HERO

"I can't drive the American economy. All I can do, to the best of my abilities with the Tánaiste and our colleagues, is to try and manage the Irish very well."

Irish Independent • 7 June 2003

OPPOSITES ATTRACT!

"Of course, we differ in various policy areas, but that is not to say we should not be working closely together."

(Talking about links between the
EU and the United States)

Irish Independent • 3 January 2004

SO IT'S NOT TRUE THEN?

"I suppose in the most friendly way it's all nonsense, one hundred per cent incorrect, it's all one hundred per cent inaccurate and it's also offensive. Charlie is my closest colleague in the cabinet."

(On Charlie McCreevy's move to Brussels)

Irish Independent • 22 July 2004

TOUGH ON CRIME!

"There's one way I've always believed in – in dealing with crime – and that's the tough end of it."

Sunday Independent • 26 November 2006

AND THE CAUSES OF CRIME!

"The reality is that if young people do not get a bit of a rough time from the police, we will never address these issues."

(On hooliganism)

Sunday Independent • 17 April 2005

DOWN WITH THE KIDS!

"If a child of 14 tries one fag or one drink it doesn't make them a compulsive smoker or an alcoholic."

The Irish Times • 1 March 2007

PROGRESSIVE COMMENTS

"I passionately believe that making progress in the shorter term is the best course. But the facts are very simple. If everybody sticks to their present position, there is no hope I can do it."

(Baffling for Europe while President of the European Council)

Sunday Independent • 18 January 2004

A TRUE SPORTS FAN

"I love reading the sports pages. At least you know what's in them is true, unlike the rest of the papers."

Irish Independent • 3 February 2005

SAUCER OF MILK!

"I know the show is being done kind of as a show for the audience. A lot of it has been based on putting on a presentation, rather than always being factual."

(On Eddie Hobbs' 'Rip Off Republic')

Sunday Independent • 4 September 2005

WHY ME?

*"As always, as party leader,
I'm left to sort it out."*

(Talking about errant Fianna Fáil TD)

Irish Independent • 27 December 2003

GRAVE DIGGERS

"There was one group out to bury me, very persistently to bury me."

(On the payments controversy)

Sunday Independent • 12 November 2006

DIGGING DEEPER!

"I'd love to know. And I'd bury them. But I don't know. But somebody was. Somebody had fairly calculated and manipulatively planned this out."

(Referring to the leaks which led
to the payments controversy)

Sunday Independent • 24 December 2006

THANKS FOR THE TIP!

"It's important to find the right balance between being able to remember a lot of information and being able to analyse what you know."

(On the Leaving Cert)

Sunday Independent • 11 June 2006

CHEQUE MATE

"The vast, vast majority of cheques that I had signed were used for appropriate purposes. A smaller group of them weren't. That's regrettable."

(On the Moriarty Tribunal's findings that he signed blank cheques for Charles Haughey)

Sunday Tribune • 24 December 2006

CHECKING OUT!

"History's ultimate judgement on Mr Haughey will be a positive one."

(On the death of Charles Haughey)

The People • 18 June 2006

BETTER RETURNS!

"*I think now that will be gone and an awful lot of decent people will go back into them and I think they will make more money, even though most of them are making too much anyway.*"

(On the introduction of smoke free pubs)

Sunday Independent • 2 November 2003

THAT'S TELLING THEM!

"I will not just click my fingers because some right wing economists believe we should privatise Aer Lingus."

Sunday Tribune • 21 November 2004

PRE-BUDGET FORECAST

*"We won't do anything zany.
We will continue to be prudent."*

(On the Budget)

Irish Independent • 12 November 2006

ALL FOR ONE AND ONE FOR ALL!

"I head a government that is a collective government. Everybody works together. The one thing that I do not allow is people thinking that they have personal fiefdoms."

Sunday Independent • 10 September 2006

FAST FOOD NATIONALISTS?

"There are kebabs out there plotting against us."

(Telling Fianna Fáil members to be wary of cabals plotting against them)

Sunday Independent • 4 January 2004

Bertie-isms

DUCK!

"I don't think it helps people to start throwing white elephants and red herrings at each other."

Questions and Answers • RTÉ • 28 March 1994

DON'T ASK ME!

"My own personal position is irrelevant in this."

(Going into coalition with Labour)

Farrell • RTÉ • 20 November 1994

PICK OF THE CROP

"And you can't find money on trees."

Questions and Answers • RTÉ • 28 March 1994

NOTHIN' PERSONAL, LIKE

"There's no point in personalising any of the people involved in this."

Questions and Answers • RTÉ • 7 December 1992

BAD ROLE MODELS?

"I'd go and buy meself a country home or an offshore island or something like that."

(On winning the Lottery)

RTÉ News • 22 March 1987

BENEFIT OF THE DOUBT?

"Armed both with revolvers, pistols and baseball bats, and I suppose we could all conclude that, whatever they were about, they were up to no good."

(Talking about Real IRA arrests)

Oireachtas Report • RTÉ • 31 January 2001

AERIAL ATTACK!

"A fly-past shooting."

(Describing a gangland shoot-out
on Dublin's M50 motorway)

The Irish Times • 1 April 2006

OPPOSITION OPTIONS

"Now we will be an aggressive Opposition where we oppose things and we'll support things that we support."

RTÉ News • 26 September 1995

STATING THE OBVIOUS

"Every party knows that the composition of the next government will be determined by the electorate."

Sunday Independent • 31 December 2000

POLL POSITION

"I think every opinion poll is just a snapshot of events at any particular time."

The Irish Times • 21 November 2000

HUMBLE PIE

"(They)... are trying to upset the apple tart."

The Irish Times Magazine • 19 May 2001

ALL THE WORLD'S
A STAGE

*"You only have one life.
This isn't a rehearsal."*

The Late Late Show • RTÉ • 25 May 2001

TERMINATOR TOO

*"The grass roots, or the rank and file,
are now made from fibre-optics."*

The Irish Times • 7 March 1995

INDIGESTION

"We all have to swallow humble pie, and I have been doing it for years, but if you keep at it, you can break through and get selected at the convention."

The Irish Times • 21 November 1994

MAN OF THE PEOPLE

"... I came up through the people system."

The Irish Times • 5 June 1997

DIRT TRIBUNAL

"Let's put the dirty linen, the clean linen on the table — deal with them — Take the recommendations..."

Later with O'Leary • RTÉ • 31 May 2000

BOOM TIMES!

"In actual fact, the reason it's on the rise is because probably the boom times are getting even more boomer."

(On the success of the Irish economy)

Sunday Independent • 16 July 2006

TEMPORARY CEASEFIRE

"Those groups who are not on ceasefire or even maybe those who are on ceasefire at the edges might be involved in some activities."

(at the Fianna Fáil Ard-Fheis)

RTÉ News • 4 March 2000

URBAN GUERRILLAS

"Charles J. Haughey wanted to transform Temple Bar into Ireland's West Bank."

The Irish Times Magazine • 19 May 2001

BETTER THAN SEX

"If I can help in getting a person a house or a medical card, it is as good as scoring a goal on Sunday."

Sunday Press • 24 February 1983

LIMBO DANCING

"In political life, you have a hassle period of some difficulties. I'm neither separated nor totally the best family man in the world. I'm in between."

In Dublin • 10 April 1991

TIME TRAVELLERS

"There's one thing I can't do...
I can't change the past..."

RTÉ News • 15 October 1997

... and later in same interview...

"All 'at we're trying to do is to
clean up the past..."

"The cynics may be able to point to the past
but we live in the future — *and we work for*
the future."

Fianna Fáil Ard-Fheis 1998

MAYBE... MAYBE NOT...

"It's a matter that an awful lot of people want or maybe an awful lot of people don't want and the people will decide ultimately."

(on Divorce)

Kenny Live • RTÉ • 17 November 1994

"People setting deadlines is always difficult... I'd rather not tie myself to an exact week or date."

(on Abortion)

Irish Examiner • 22 January 2000

SURE EVERYBODY WAS AT IT!

"If I ever for a moment had thought that by signing a cheque, which was a practice that everybody did in the country, let's be very frank and honest about it and let's not be prudish about it, I would never have signed them."

(Referring to the Moriarty Tribunal findings)

Sunday Independent • 24 December 2006

SPLITTING HAIRS

"If hindsight were foresight, there wouldn't be a problem..."

(on his Moriarty Tribunal evidence)

The Irish Times • 30 June 2000

A TRUE DEMOCRAT

"It is no good in politics devising policies that do not have the support of the people and cannot win the support of the people."

The Irish Times • 13 May 1997

PASS THE WAFFLES

"You're a waffler, a waffler — and you've always been a waffler."

(in Dáil confrontation with Gay Mitchell)

Quoted in
Bertie Ahern — Taoiseach and Peacemaker

SO *THAT'S* WHAT THEY DO!

"One thing that she did very successfully...
she kept in touch with all the people in the
country. She spent six months going around...
and I would hope that in her seven years,
that she keeps that up because
I think it is important."

(on Mary Robinson's election)

Questions and Answers • RTÉ • 12 November 1990

SEVEN YEAR HITCH!

"I think too many people who commit murders get out after seven years and personally I think it's too long............personally I think it's too short, I should say."

(A little confused following a shooting)

The Irish Times • 11 March 2006

HI, MY NAME IS...

"Well ministers... regularly — and this is a good thing in this democracy — meet people. It is a very good idea, I think, for ministers to meet people."

Prime Time • RTÉ • 26 January 1999

Bertie-isms

and

Haughey

WISHFUL THINKING

"I'd love to see Haughey get an overall majority; it's about the only thing that he hasn't achieved. I think if he got that, within a few years he would go."

In Dublin • 10 April 1991

STAND BY YER MAN

"I have been a supporter of Mr Haughey for as long as I have been in politics... I think he has been an excellent leader of this country – some people might disagree – and they're quite entitled to disagree — and he has said in his judgment when he feels it's time to go that he'll go...and I think he will go."

Questions and Answers • RTÉ • 21 October 1991

EXCELLENT
MISJUDGEMENT

"His judgement on the vast majority of issues has been excellent."

(On Haughey)

Questions and Answers • RTÉ • 21 October 1991

MIND YER HEAD!

"Personally, of course, I do not want to see any more fall on the head of Charlie Haughey. He's a good man who served the country well and I think he's taken a lot of knocks and he is getting older."

The Irish Times • 5 January 1998

SPLIT PERSONALITY

"You had to put your personality to one side and say that there were things he did that were not correct."

The Irish Sun • 14 May 2001

AND THE
DIFFERENCE IS…?

"I did not distance myself from him. I distanced myself from what I believe are unacceptable practices."

The Irish Times • 13 May 1997

COMMITTED
FENCE-SITTING

"I gave equal credit and equal blame to Charles Haughey's role and I stand over those things."

Later with O'Leary • RTÉ • 31 May 2000

REALLY?

"I would never condemn wrongdoing."

Sunday Tribune • 31 December 2006

YER HISTORY, PAL!

"I think Charlie Haughey is basically a very good man and unfortunately he got into things like the lifestyle. And the bills around the lifestyle required him to do some things that I feel very strongly about. But I actually think history will be kind to him."

The Irish Sun • 14 May 2001

The Ahern Years 1

BEFORE BERTIE	**AFTER BERTIE**
CJH	*CJD*
FLAT CAP	*FLAT SCREEN*
PRO-LIFE	*WESTLIFE*
EASI-SINGLES	*MOZZARELLA*
HORSLIPS	*COLLAGEN IMPLANTS*

What he Said...
Rough Translations

WHAT HE SAID

"I, however, am a Dubliner who was born on a farm. My father was the farm manager at All Hallowes College in Dublin. I understand and respect farming as a way of life."

The Irish Times • 19 May 1997

ROUGH TRANSLATION

I love culchies – just give me yer bleedin' vote!

WHAT HE SAID

"(I understand) the problems of people – people in factories and on farms, in small businesses, at home, in schools and communities."

The Irish Times • 5 June 1997

ROUGH TRANSLATION

I love everyone – just give me yer bleedin' vote!

WHAT HE SAID

"Nobody in this country is too rich, too powerful or too important to escape detection and investigation."

(on Tax Dodgers)

The Irish Times • 5 January 1998

ROUGH TRANSLATION

...And when we find them, we'll give them another amnesty.

WHAT HE SAID

"I would have stronger views than most people."

Evening Herald • 5 May 1998

ROUGH TRANSLATION

...I just don't know what they are...

WHAT HE SAID

"*I think it is good that we have a debate on the issue. We have stuck with our system for a long time. Perhaps following the debate, we will end up with exactly the same system.*"

(on Electoral Reform)

The Irish Times • 20 October 1999

ROUGH TRANSLATION

Go ahead and have your debate...
I'll do as I please anyway.

WHAT HE SAID

"If it was Fianna Fáil on their own, I'd be happy. If it's Fianna Fáil and the PDs, I'll be happy. And if it's Fianna Fáil, the PDs and the Independents, I'll be happy. I'll work with what the people decide. Any of those will be better than losing."

The Irish Sun • 14 May 2001

ROUGH TRANSLATION

I'd go into power with anyone!

WHAT HE SAID

"I want to see the party getting down to the problems of family law and other social policy... the accountability of public funds and ensuring that the State's money is properly spent..."

Sunday Press • 24 February 1983

ROUGH TRANSLATION

You mean we'll actually have to do something?

WHAT HE SAID

"One of the great things Haughey has is that he knows so many things. On the Cabinet table, that really comes across."

In Dublin • 10 April 1991

ROUGH TRANSLATION

Haughey knows everything... except, of course, where his money comes from.

WHAT HE SAID

"... Just a way that things went on that was not an acceptable way — they maybe strictly weren't illegal but that was stretching the law... We brought in an enormous amount of laws and legislation. But things are different now — and I think we've cleaned up politics."

The Late Late Show • RTÉ • 25 May 2001

ROUGH TRANSLATION

We can't get away with it anymore... so we've been forced to clean up politics...

WHAT HE SAID

*"All of us, including Fianna Fáil, have found
ourselves in politically embarrassing situations
or controversies, from which lessons have
had to be learned."*

The Irish Times • 4 June 1998

ROUGH TRANSLATION

Just don't get caught!

WHAT HE SAID

"*I won an essay competition when I was 13, on the title 'When I'll be Taoiseach'. I don't know if that was an ambition or what it was. I don't think I have that ambition now.*"

Evening Herald • 2 November 1989

ROUGH TRANSLATION

I want to be Taoiseach!

WHAT HE SAID

"*I had a huge interest in the Paris riots in '68 and Ché Guevara and the Chilean revolution, you name it. But once I got interested in Fianna Fáil, I stuck with it and kept working away.*"

Evening Herald • 2 November 1989

ROUGH TRANSLATION

I'm boring... I'm an accountant... but I have to make myself sound interesting.

WHAT HE SAID

"Sports Campus Ireland... is a part of that vision. It's a small part in one way, and a huge part in another."

The Irish Times • 27 January 2000

ROUGH TRANSLATION

It's trivial compared to hospital waiting lists, but it will be a huge part of our spending.

WHAT HE SAID

"I made Fianna Fáil's position very clear at the Ard-Fheis. Nobody could read any ambiguous signs into it."

(on Haughey)

The Irish Times • 13 May 1997

ROUGH TRANSLATION

I hope nobody has a clue what I'm talking about...

WHAT HE SAID

"*We must stop listening to the do-gooders who have all the excuses and all the problems.*"

The Irish Times • 7 March 1995

ROUGH TRANSLATION

We'll have to listen to Charlie McCreevy instead.

WHAT HE SAID

"If getting there means selling your soul a little bit, there isn't a profession in the world where you don't have to change your principles."

The Irish Times • 21 November 1994

ROUGH TRANSLATION

Principles? What principles?

Just What the Hell is He Talking About?

"It is as complicated or as simple as that, whatever way you want to put it. If you look at the complications, they are horrendous. Potentially, you could have trouble here, there and everywhere."

The Irish Times • 22 January 1999

What's he talking about:

(A) Failing the Leaving Cert
(B) Being Taoiseach
(C) The Middle East
(D) Making a Decision

Answer (C)

"It's about getting the business done, obtaining the right results. It's not about the preaching to the converted, but convincing the unpersuaded. It's not about telling them what to do, but leading them to see themselves what needs to be done, if necessary, in their own time."

Sunday Independent • 31 December 2000

What's he talking about:

(A) Teaching
(B) Training Junior Footballers
(C) Effective Political Leadership
(D) Pulling the Perfect Pint

Answer (C)

"We prepared the ground and cut the grass for them. Some of their stuff just sticks in my gullet."

Sunday Tribune • 19 November 1989

What's he talking about:

(A) Junior Soccer Opponents
(B) The Local Chipper
(C) Farmers
(D) Employers

Answer (D)

"It is our belief that the whole matter can be dealt with in three months."

RTÉ News • 3 September 1997

What's he talking about:

(A) Decommissioning
(B) The Planning Tribunal
(C) My Wardrobe
(D) Deciding What to Have for Breakfast

Answer (B)

Bertie's Inner Self

LOVE

*"I hate nobody and am never angry
at people for long.
Life's too short."*

The Irish Sun • 14 May 2001

MATERIAL THINGS

*"The only things I always have in my wallet
are the St Francis Xavier Novena of Grace
Prayer and Programme...
and the Man. United fixtures list."*

Evening Herald • 5 May 1998

HAPPINESS

"When people are happy, I'm happy."

The Late Late Show • RTÉ • 25 May 2001

NIRVANA

*"If I have enough to go to a match and have
a few pints and a holiday and get
over to United a few times a year and
a few race meetings, I'm happy."*

The Irish Sun • 14 May 2001

STRESS

"I just like to be straight. Otherwise it gets to me. And if something gets to me inside, then I can't operate."

Evening Herald • 5 May 1998

NEGATIVITY

"...*Type of Creeping Jesus...*"

"*For Christ sakes, let us not get carried away
by all the negative talk.*"

Irish Independent • 8 April 2000

The Ahern Years 2

BEFORE BERTIE	AFTER BERTIE
P&T	IT
LADA	PRADA
EARLY HOUSE	PENTHOUSE
MEDICAL CARD	GOLD CARD
STRIKES	STRIKES

The World According to Celia

DON'T FORGET, NOW!

"Sleep every night. Nothing will make you more irritable than lack of sleep."

Irish Mirror • 20 December 2000

LOITERING WITH INTENT

"In the weeks... or days before the interview, go and have a look at what the other employees and your (hopefully future) employer wear to work. Watch them going into the workplace in the morning or leaving at lunchtime."

Irish Mirror • 14 June 2000

I WISH I'D LOOKED AFTER ME FEET

"The Christmas Party season, particularly after-work drinks parties, means lots of standing around. So take care of your feet by giving yourself a foot massage."

Irish Mirror • 20 December 2000

WALKING THE WALK...

"Why not try a walk in the fresh air? Walking is free and if you walk at a reasonably fast pace, you will burn off calories, stimulate your circulation and build up your stamina."

Irish Mirror • 12 July 2000

A GOOD INVESTMENT

"If you meet people outdoors, then spend money on your overcoat."

Irish Mirror • 31 May 2000

IT'S HARDER THAN YOU THINK

"Discipline, control and balance are the keys to good shopping, and good shopping is an acquired skill."

Irish Mirror • 31 May 2000

POETRY IN MOTION

"... And what about those long skirts with the split up the back?... Well, the skirt divides at the back and catches between your legs at the front, exposing cellulite and flab on the inner thigh... So always check the view from behind, not just when standing still but when you are in motion."

Irish Mirror • 26 April 2001

The Ahern Years 3

BEFORE BERTIE

UNITED IRELAND

BRYLCREEM

MOBILE HOME

COMMIES

FORD CORTINA

AFTER BERTIE

MAN UNITED

WAX

MOBILE PHONE

DOT COM

BMW-7 SERIES

DIY BERTIE
SPEECH-MAKING 1

*WORDS NEEDED FOR A
TYPICAL BERTIE SPEECH*

People
Electorate
Statistics ("Satistics")
Criticism ("Crisicism")
Things ("Tings")
Growth ("Growt")
Citizens ("Sitisens")
Join ("Jain")
Doing ("Doin")
Competitiveness ("Competi-ness")

DIY BERTIE
SPEECH-MAKING 2

*PHRASES NEEDED FOR A
TYPICAL BERTIE SPEECH*

"I have no difficulty..."
"In the national interest..."
"My own personal opinion is irrelevant."
"At the end of the day..."
"Bring the parties together..."
"Deal with the issues..."
"I have great respect..."
"It's up to them."
"It will be dealt with in time."
"Terms of reference..."

Other Famous Berties

BERTIE THE BEET

A sugar beet called Bertie has his own cult website. The beet was originally a footnote in a weekly Internet bulletin for British Beet-growers – but Bertie's progress from a seedling to a 20-inch plant attracted fans worldwide. A website www.bertiethebeet.co.uk was set up. Unfortunately, Bertie the Beet was dug up for sugar in October 2001.

BERTIE THE BUS

Bertie the Bus is a friend of the children's animated cartoon character, Thomas the Tank Engine. Bertie's strongest characteristics are his friendly grin and his readiness to help any engine prepared to admit that – just sometimes – roads have their uses as well as rails.